W9-COG-222

Puppies

● ANIMAL BABIES SERIES ●

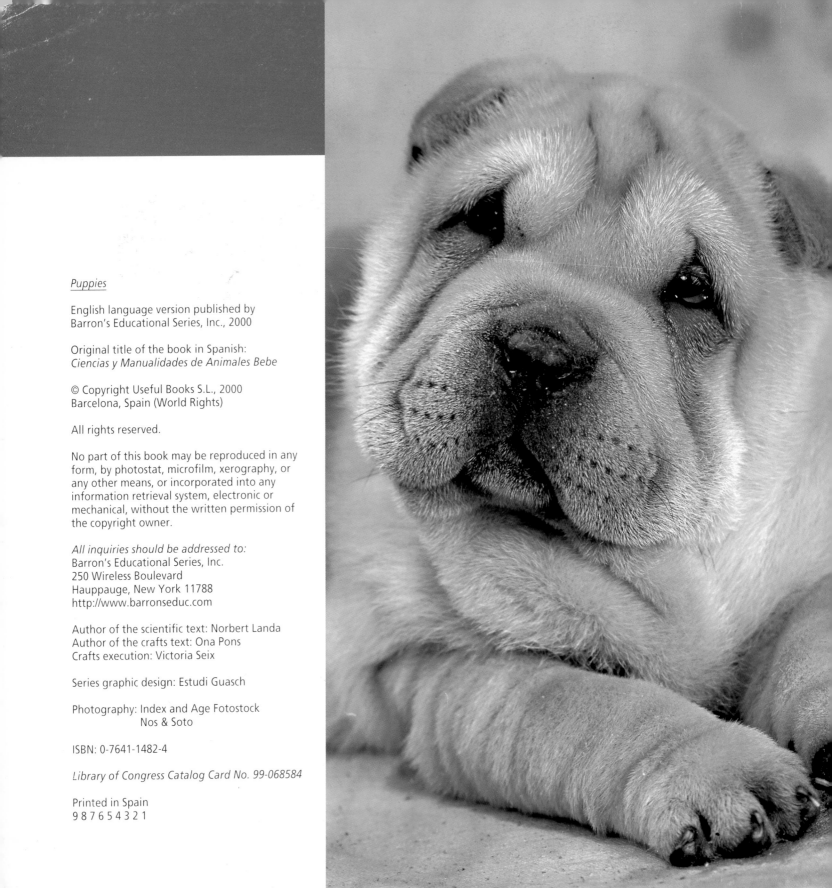

Puppies

English language version published by
Barron's Educational Series, Inc., 2000

Original title of the book in Spanish:
Ciencias y Manualidades de Animales Bebe

© Copyright Useful Books S.L., 2000
Barcelona, Spain (World Rights)

All rights reserved.

No part of this book may be reproduced in any
form, by photostat, microfilm, xerography, or
any other means, or incorporated into any
information retrieval system, electronic or
mechanical, without the written permission of
the copyright owner.

All inquiries should be addressed to:
Barron's Educational Series, Inc.
250 Wireless Boulevard
Hauppauge, New York 11788
http://www.barronseduc.com

Author of the scientific text: Norbert Landa
Author of the crafts text: Ona Pons
Crafts execution: Victoria Seix

Series graphic design: Estudi Guasch

Photography: Index and Age Fotostock
                        Nos & Soto

ISBN: 0-7641-1482-4

Library of Congress Catalog Card No. 99-068584

Printed in Spain
9 8 7 6 5 4 3 2 1

Puppies

Facts:

Fun:

Do you like dogs

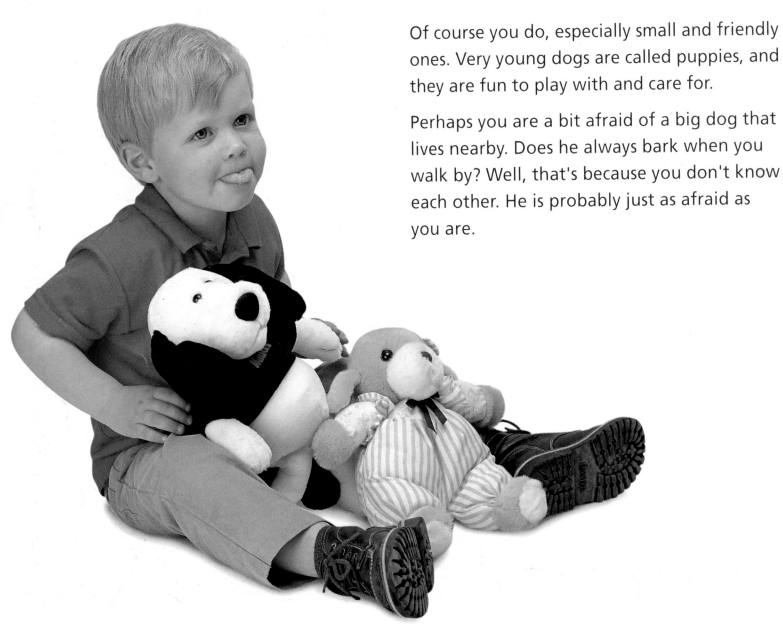

Of course you do, especially small and friendly ones. Very young dogs are called puppies, and they are fun to play with and care for.

Perhaps you are a bit afraid of a big dog that lives nearby. Does he always bark when you walk by? Well, that's because you don't know each other. He is probably just as afraid as you are.

How many kinds of dogs are there

There are many, many kinds of dogs. Some are as small as your shoe, even when they are all grown up. Some dogs can grow as big as ponies. Some have very short legs, others have very long legs. Some look as fierce as a wolf, but others are as cute as your teddy bear.

Are dogs domestic or wild?

Did you know that dogs are related to some wild animals such as wolves, foxes, and jackals? These animals are not used to being around people, so they usually run away from them.

Dogs are used to living among people, so you can keep them at home.
Some dogs help people to herd sheep, or hunt, or just protect their homes.

In return, their masters feed them and take care of them.

Puppies

What do puppies eat

Puppies need to drink their mother's milk for the first few weeks of life.
They cannot eat meat or chew bones when they are little, so their mom takes care of them.

Puppies soon start growing big and strong, and as they play they learn about the outside world. Their mother teaches them how to behave like dogs.

How do puppies talk

Puppies communicate by barking, making faces and wagging their tails.

Would you like to know some words in dog language?

Wagging the tail means "Hello, I like you!"

Putting down the tail means "I am afraid."

Pricking up the ears means "I'm listening and trying to understand."

Letting down the ears means "I am so sad!"

What happens when puppies grow up

Soon your puppy will grow up and become an adult dog. But just like when he was a pup, he needs healthy food, a good friend to walk him once or twice a day, and someone to give him a bath, take him to the veterinarian, play with him, and make him feel loved and wanted.

What do puppies have to learn

Dogs have to learn how to behave in the world of humans, and we have to start teaching them when they are just puppies. For example, they need to learn not to hide bones under the carpet, not to chew the furniture, how to become house–trained, not to scare children or chase the mailman, not to run away from home, not to bark all night long ...

A well-trained dog makes life easier for everybody.

Are you ready to take care of a puppy

If you would like to have a puppy, or you already have one, you must know that he or she is a living being that needs love, care, and time. Even the smallest and cutest puppy will grow up and become an adult dog.

Having a dog also involves your entire family. You alone would not be able to give your puppy all he needs for the next 15 years or so. Besides, you cannot just return a dog!

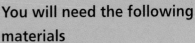

You will need the following materials

Cloth (blue, white, black, green, yellow, and orange),
Velcro,
a hole puncher,
a pencil, scissors,
and white glue.

A Dalmatian who is always with you will never feel lonely!

A Dalmatian pencil bag

1 Duplicate the Dalmatian template on page 31 over the white cloth, the bushes on the green cloth, and the flowers on the yellow and orange cloths.

20

2 Cut out a square of blue cloth, big enough to hold pencils and the other outlined pieces. Add a few clouds.

3 To make the black spots for your Dalmatian, punch holes in the black cloth using the hole puncher.

4 Fold the square of blue cloth in half; use some white glue to hold the sides together and to attach all other pieces that you cut out. Let everything dry.

5 Attach some Velcro on the inside upper part of the pencil bag.
Your pencil bag will be the most original one in the class.

You will need the following materials:

Two large matchboxes,
two plastic containers for camera
film, tissue paper (orange, yellow,
red, white, and black),
scissors, a stick of glue,
adhesive tape, yellow
and orange paper necklaces.

A Cocker Spaniel puppet

Can you make a Cocker Spaniel bark?

1 Cut out one side of one of the inside boxes. Cut the corners off the other box and unfold the flaps.

2 Separate the flaps of the cut-out side to make the tongue and glue it to the outside box.

3 Use tape to attach the two plastic film containers to the outside box.

4 Tear pieces of orange tissue paper and glue them to the boxes. Make the face and the tongue red. Make small balls with black tissue paper for the eyes and the nose.

5 Cut two equal lengths of paper necklace, fold them in half and hold both ends together with tape. Use a piece of tissue paper to tie them to the head.

6 Fit the folded side of the upper box between the lower boxes; it will be the hinge that will allow you to make your dog open its mouth.

7 If you place your thumb in the lower box and your other fingers in the upper box, you only have to open and close your hand to make your cocker spaniel bark!

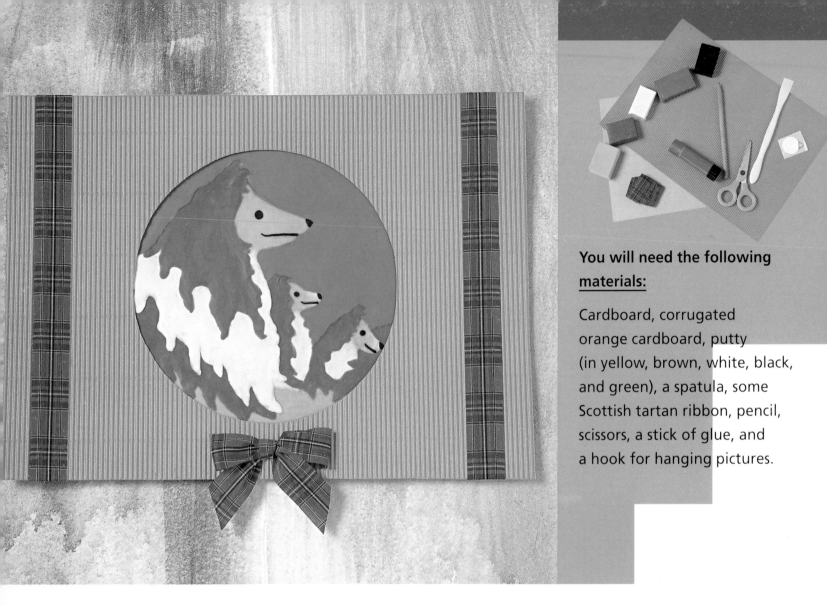

Cardboard, corrugated orange cardboard, putty (in yellow, brown, white, black, and green), a spatula, some Scottish tartan ribbon, pencil, scissors, a stick of glue, and a hook for hanging pictures.

Mother Collie takes care of her family.

A Collie family portrait

1 On a piece of cardboard, trace the family of Collies. The template appears on page 31.

2 Cover the outlines drawn with the putty, smoothing it with your fingers and trying to spread it thin. Use the spatula to adjust the outlines.

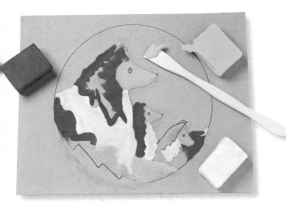

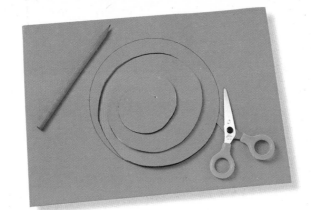

3 From the corrugated cardboard, cut out a circle that is just slightly smaller than the one decorated with the putty.

4 Glue the corrugated cardboard over the decorated cardboard to make the frame of your portrait.

5 Decorate the corrugated cardboard by gluing two pieces of ribbon to the sides and a bow in the center. Attach a hook to the back so you can hang your portrait.

6 You now have a nice picture to hang in your room or to give as a present to a friend who likes dogs as much as you do.

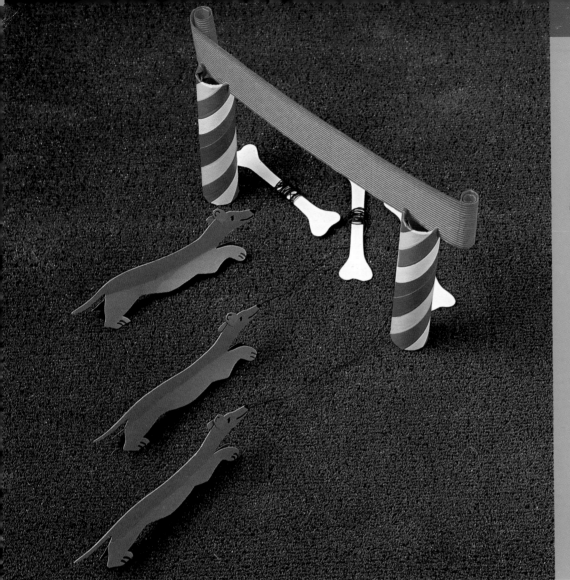

You will need the following materials:

Bristol board (brown and white), string, a pencil, scissors, a stick of glue, and
a black marker.

These puppies are now old enough to start eating bones.

A Dachshund race

1 On a piece of brown bristol board, trace the outline of the Dachshund and its ear twice, using the template on page 30. On a piece of white bristol board trace the outline of the bone, also twice.

2 Cut out all the pieces carefully.

3 Extend a line of glue from the head to the tail. Attach one end of the string to the middle of the head and glue the other side of the dog over it.

4 Attach the ears, one to each side of the dog. Glue both parts of the bone together with the other end of the string in the middle.

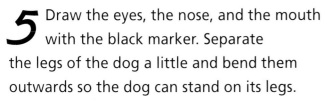

5 Draw the eyes, the nose, and the mouth with the black marker. Separate the legs of the dog a little and bend them outwards so the dog can stand on its legs.

6 Place the dog on the ground, pull the string, and roll it around the bone. The dog will move forward. Make as many Dachshunds as you want and race your friends!

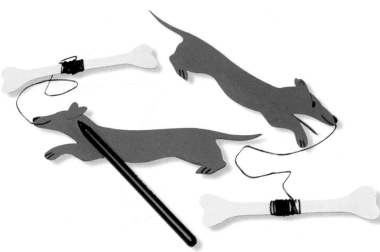

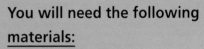

You will need the following materials:

Crepe paper (yellow, brown, white, black, pink, and purple), scissors, a pencil, and a stick of glue.

If you wear one, no one will take you for a wild dog.

A Yorkshire Terrier mask

1 Fold in half two squares of yellow crepe paper, each bigger than your head. Draw and cut out an outline like in the picture.

2 Spread some glue all around one of the cutout figures, except at the bottom. Place the other figure over it and press to glue.

3 Try the mask on and carefully mark the place where the eyes go. Take the mask off and cut out the holes for the eyes.

4 Cut strips of white, yellow, and brown crepe paper to make a fringe of bangs. Make the strips thinner and longer for the moustache and front tuft.

5 Cut out two ears (pink), a tongue (red), a strip for the mouth (also red), and a longer strip (purple) for the bow. Make the nose with a ball of black crepe paper.

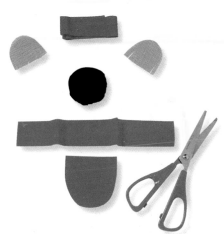

6 Put some glue on the pieces and attach them to the mask. Start with the mouth and then add both ears, the side strips, and the beard. Now attach the front tuft and the moustache.

7 Add the nose, the tongue, and finally attach some strips to the back of the mask and the bow to the front tuft.

Templates

Place some tracing paper over the template you want to copy. Trace the outline with a pencil. Turn the tracing paper over and retrace the outline over the chosen bristol or cardboard.

A Dachshund race, page 26

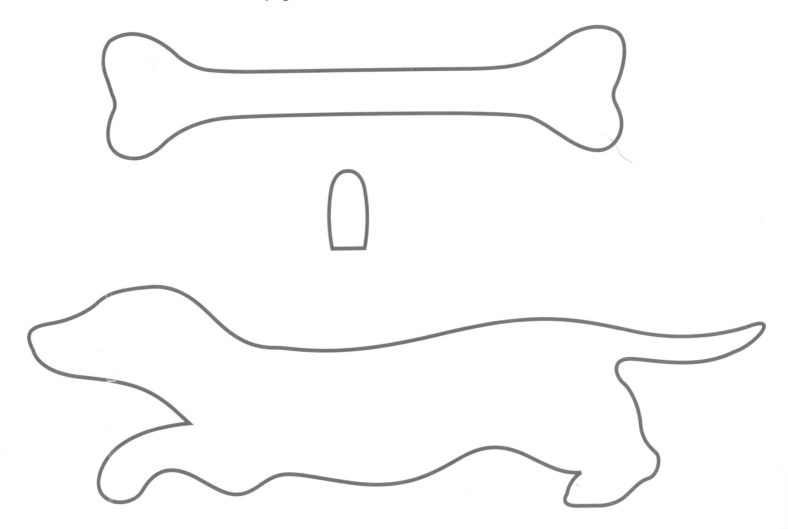

A Dalmatian pencil bag, page 20

A Collie family portrait, page 24

Can my puppy fly?
No, and nor can I.

Can my puppy moo?
No, but I can do.

Can my puppy sing a song?
No, but he can howl along.

Can my puppy chew a shoe?
Yes, but that I wouldn't do.

Now I'm telling you
what we both can do:

Both of us know how
to make bow wow, bow wow!

My puppy and I